SHUT UP SHUT DOWN

Poems by Mark Nowak

AFTERWORD BY AMIRI BARAKA

COFFEE HOUSE PRESS

Minneapolis

2004

Coffee House Press books are available to the trade through our primary distributor, Consortium Book Sales & Distribution, 1045 Westgate Drive, Saint Paul, MN 55114. For personal orders, catalogs, or other information, write to: Coffee House Press, 27 North Fourth Street, Suite 400, Minneapolis, MN 55401.

Coffee House Press is a nonprofit literary publishing house. Support from private foundations, corporate giving programs, government programs, and generous individuals help make the publication of our books possible. We gratefully acknowledge their support in detail in the back of this book.

LIBRARY OF CONGRESS CATALOGING-IN-PUBLICATION DATA
Nowak, Mark, 1964—
Shut up shut down / Mark Nowak.
p. cm.
ISBN 1-56689-163-9 (alk. paper)
1. Corporations—Corrupt practices—Literary collections.
2. Corporate culture—Literary collections.
3. Business ethics—Literary collections.
4. Greed—Literary collections.
I. Title. OS3614.096S55 2004
813'.54—DC22
2004012789

5 7 9 8 6 4
Printed in the United States

ACKNOWLEDGMENTS

$00 / Line / Steel / Train was originally published in the "Writing (Working) Class" issue of *Xcp: Cross Cultural Poetics* (no. 9); an excerpt appears in *Working Words: A Working Class and Labor Literary Reader* (Wayne State University Press, 2005), edited by M. L. Liebler.

Capitalization was awarded a Downstage Left development grant and premiered on George Washington's Birthday (February 22, 2004) at Stage Left Theatre in Chicago (Eric Reda, director). The first six sections appeared as the inaugural *winteRed* chaplet (thanks to Sun Yung Shin and Rachel Moritz); other sections appeared in *The Butchershop* (thanks to Simon Morrison).

June 19, 1982 appeared in *markszine* <http://www.markszine.com> out of Detroit (thanks to Deborah King, Ted Pearson, Sheila Lloyd, Dennis Teichman, and M. L. Liebler for making Detroit a little closer to home) and *LVNG* (thanks to Peter O'Leary).

Francine Michalek Drives Bread premiered at the UAW Local 879 union hall in St. Paul, Minnesota, on March 27, 2003, as part of the Radical History Conference/Culture @ Work program (May Mahala, director); an excerpt appeared in *Chicago Review* (thanks to Eirik Steinhoff, Matthias Regan, and Eric Elshtain).

Hoyt Lakes / Shut Down appeared in the "Global/Local" issue of *Tripwire* (no. 7); a letterpress chapbook version was published by State Street Press (thanks to David Buuck, Yedda Morrison, and Paulette Myers-Rich).

Extra thanks to everyone at Coffee House Press, without whose support this book simply would not exist; to Peter Rachleff and the St. Paul Labor Speakers Club, who keep social movement unionism alive in the Upper Midwest; to the founding collective of the Union of Radical Workers and Writers (Jason Evans, Holly Krig, and Sun Yung Shin), who help me keep Subcommandante Marcos's idea that "The war for the word has begun" alive in diverse struggles both on the page and in the streets; to Wang Ping and Maria Damon for energizing conversations on how to historicize, critique, and expand radical working class and anti-imperialist literatures locally and globally; to the poets from "The Social Mark"; and to my family, my extended family, and my co-workers across the globe.

CONTENTS

$00 / LINE / STEEL / TRAIN

1.

The basic form is the frame; the photograph of the factory predicts how every one (of the materials) will get used. **and I can remember Mark & I talking about the possibility of Lackawanna becoming a ghost town** Past (participle) past (participant) past (articulating) an incessant scraping (away). **and what would we do. You know—it wasn't just losing a job in the steel industry, but your entire life, the place that you grew up in was going to be gone.** As I scraped (grease, meat, omelettes), the (former) railroad workers and steel workers (still) bullshitting in the restaurant where for eight years I short-order cooked.

*

Who knew

the crisis

from the conditions—

presumably
the Capital [Who]

2.

Built sheds and piss houses. We took care of shit. Nation ("Under Construction") needs the State (in decay)—a flag out of focus where working-class (white) masculinity also factors into how factories get framed. **You made steel together and you won your dignity together.** Inside my third-grade (Union Road) classroom, the distant bay of trains (braking) out behind Buffalo Salvage & Tow. All those present (in prefigured relations) are constituted for a State that will remain (for us) always German-shepherd guarded. **You couldn't make steel alone and you couldn't win respect alone.** Further up the road was the Local.

*

Bricks, the frame [work]
of an eye, accents
of bricklayer

and optometrist, tongues
extant

13.

of the sequence?

The interruption of the closure, in this instance, by the frame: "LTV [Steel] was able to use its bankruptcy to reduce payments to productive workers." **In the old days when the city bus used to pull up to the factory gate, the driver would call out "butcher shop" or "slaughterhouse."** "In negotiations with the steelworkers union, LTV extracted more takebacks than other, presumably healthier steel companies were able to." **I can remember sitting around the lunch table and everybody at that table, there must have been seven or eight people, had a finger or something missing.** "This gave LTV an advantage over its competitors." **Believe it or not, people felt it was kind of like a badge of honor that they had a finger or something missing, and that would be a topic of conversation.** "Bankruptcy became, through a cultural process that understood bankruptcy as failure, a condition for success."

*

Where are

yards   our

yards where our

no you cannot

yards [where] away

38.

They put me in hot places all summer, where not many men will stay; when it gets cool they layed [sic] me off; White men get my job . . . I have went to see the employment manager of the mill [and] all he says is their [sic] is no call for colored men. He has sent me to places in the mill where I have worked as good as any other man, but I can't get the job steady, on account of I am not [a] White man . . . I don't think it fair . . . I have a right to a living as well as anyone else, no matter what color I am . . . The basic form (the photograph of a factory inside this frame) does not discontinue.

*

                         Separate in/to
two tracks   two doors
                             doesn't America "Land

of the Free . . ."
    know this two from history

77.

It was a mill town, he says, singing "mill" with a blend of affection and pity. A trace (far removed): my grandfather stepping off the Clinton Street bus and into a Kaisertown gin mill, Bethlehem Steel (still) scratched across his face. **A mill town is not a goddamn residential neighborhood.** Loading crates unloaded, oil drums bent and empty, glass shattered (past tense verbs) where the window-frames (never/the/less) remain. **When I walk on the sidewalk** (here, or hear)**, I know when it's heaving from tree roots.**

*

                    How empties
    out the mouth
                            of air—How you've

    got to learn How
        to [get] chew[ed] with your mouth closed

89.

After lunch at Lucky's Texas Red Hots I took my grandfather to the steel plant to check on his pension benefits. **U.S. Steel is getting out of the steel business and they're getting out of this community.** "Not suspecting that the category of 'Progress' is completely empty and abstract." **They've raped it, soaked it, and they're saying, Good-bye.** At this juncture the choice may be between buying the entire picture or just the frame. **We've been like sheep being led to the slaughter of unemployment, into the future without steel mills, without jobs; and our mouths have been stilled and we've had nothing to say.**

*

Where is

dispossessed

from the window

of the Am/trak
Empire Builder

92.

Doors torn away in Detroit, 1974. A picture in a frame is (still) the object here. [**The ex-steelworkers**] **will use excuses, like prejudice against mill hunks, and only make a marginal effort to salve their conscience or get the wife off their backs.** Case worker mimics gendered speech while cutting class (early). **We try to strip them bare** (steel/workers)**, and then show all the ways to look for a job—** "The 'hot' economy created three million jobs in 1996, about half of them paying minimum wages (and half of those temporary or part time)." **how they can even use the obituaries to find work.**

*

When coming to
a stop   stopping
stopping Them [when]

from continuing—
from coming to

124.

"PUSSY CRUSHER" in gray spray paint—

"WEED   PENIS   MEMBERS   BEER"   (and)
"CT FUCKED EB —> HERE"

Vocabulary is the problem—men have vulgar mouths. The "CLASS OF 2001" is responsible for these words; the owners of the trains that pass them (a block from my house, rarely on schedule) will never ride this line. **Sometimes nude pictures are all over the wall.** (These are seldom in frames.) **They don't like women working, they try to embarrass you. Men** (not available for this photograph) **don't want to acknowledge a woman's place is not just in the home.**

*

              Work from the wire
     mill [the train]
                        edged through—

     waiting, don't
        worry, Who knows

148.

If you were in a pub you talked shop. How you would do things differently if you ran the place. This struggle, in each and every instance, to make history within the conditions of Whose frame. **I mean the company was always doing things that didn't make sense.** Under just such conditions, my father ran for (and was elected) vice president of his Westinghouse union. **There were a lot of smart guys in production but the company would never let you put your ideas into effect.** A railcar (still) awaits articulation in the bottom (Right) corner of this frame.

comments on prev?

*

I know what that like

There points to/ward
somewhere else
where the working

wore you, or
you worked [whatever was worn]

154.

Forty years of hard work and what have I got to show for it? Nothing.
Aerosol cans empty in the middle of the tracks is not conducting the
train. **I can't even speak proper.** Working-class kids writing their names
on a wall that is bound to erase them. **When you're a steelworker
(laughs), you don't get to speak the same language that you would do
if you meet people in a bank or business office.** On Blackrock Bridge
(above Buffalo Creek)—where my grandfather took me fishing after he
retired from Bethlehem—someone wrote (before the train came, before
the bridge tore down) "FUCK WHITE PUNKS ON DOPE!"

*

When was fond of
making   Memorials
of the materials—

they go, history
shows, sometimes, South

160.

The men knew that they were risking their jobs in the walkout ... but they had got worked up to the point where this didn't seem so important ... They were tired of never getting promoted, and they were tired of being treated

     like dogs

          by ... White ...

               foremen ...

Get work. Get (worked) over. Get up, get worked up, get working (together) again.

          *

        Because the photo

   shows [Where]

             stairs [might] mean

    the door the next flight up's

      open*

*[except the factory's long since closed]

186.

The bowling league at Holiday Bowl started at 11:00 p.m. and we bowled after working night turn. Drove the latest model automobiles and smoked filtered cigarettes (at least on billboards we were). **We bowled until 6:00 a.m.** Working-class (white) masculinity. **Just the guys from the mills. About 60 of us went all the time. We used up half the lanes.** We used, we used up, we used up (by then). **You could also continue bowling all morning long for a buck.**

*

History, the arrow

    pointing   past

[inside this frame]—

interest at 2.9% for What
we can't afford in the first place

212.

I get so damn depressed. Something like a photograph I took at the
Czestochowa Railway Station and showed to my father several months
before he died. He was (still) working at the Valu Liquor Store. **The
world could end today, and I don't give a damn.** A city inside its frame
(smokestack and steeple). **You're fifty-three and they don't want you
anymore.** Railtracks, fences, steel. **On his jacket is an "iron-master"
emblem, which u.s. Steel awarded to the workers at Duquesne for the
mill's high productivity in 1984, the year the plant closed down.** My
mother, now working (again), took a job as parish secretary at Our Lady
of Czestochowa Church.

*

Two smokestacks
within one
frame—two's no worse

than tow, one is
whether you got anyplace to go

215.

Read the writing on the Wal-Mart. **The town has never been the same, says Frank Albert, 71 . . . whose home fell to the bulldozers.** In the U.S. Steel Gary Works yard, someone spray-painted "House of Pain" on an empty coal car. **We lost a lot of people when the West Side went. There just weren't enough homes for those who wanted to stay.** Under the (Capital) cover of darkness the "HALT!" signs go unread. **Albert is still president of the West Side Hose Co., the volunteer fire department of a neighborhood that no longer exists.** Doors (scrape), doors (stain), doors (including or only their frames). **We still have meetings, he says.**

*

How this photograph

is How the frame

became

[consumption]

   How the Other Half Lives

218.

Is this the tense is this the tension is this the tension of class (framed into form)? **History tells us that the companies hired strikebreakers, with the emphasis on "break."** Steel (scrape): someone is still living in the background. **One day my dad came home from picket duty with a gash in his head.** "Open for business. Everything must go!"

*

The Local must

engage

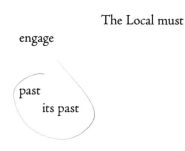

past

    its past

222.

When we were kids we thought the steel mill was it. The (scrape) wage of labor (scraping by). We'd seen the men comin' out, all dirty, black. The only thing white was the goggles over their eyes. "[S]till more important is the idea that the pleasures of whiteness could function as a 'wage' for white workers." We thought they were it, strong men. (The missing word is white.) We just couldn't wait to get in there. When we finally did get in, we were sorry. (Chuckles.) It wasn't what it was cut out to be.

*

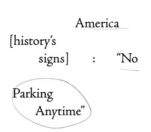

America

[history's

signs]   :   "No

Parking

Anytime"

247.

The scrape (past) of the stain. Strain (to be) of some use (value). **To strike companies that were operating at 40 percent capacity in a depressed economy amidst intensely negative public opinion would have been suicide.** Not to be: riding the train through Milwaukee, through the (back) doors of an aerosol history—a (sudden) past we wrote (again) between the lines of an oncoming train. **But many a steelworker was feeling suicidal. If need be, there might be some satisfaction to be had from one final conflagration—one final "fuck you" to the boss.**

*

In the back/ground
is the fence—

the smokestack

sans smoke [standing
   against]

257.

Because the (brake) past is used because the tearing (past) of the (brick) form is used is used because the fence (in) of the (goddamn) frame is used is used is utterly used against us and by us and upon us and for us is used is used in the present (past) future (form) we are used yet users yet used.

Every day you put your life on the line when you went into that iron house. Every day you sucked up dirt and took a chance on breaking your legs or breaking your back. And anyone who's worked in there knows what I'm talking about.

*

-roads]

Closing

words   :

[Rail

WORKS CITED

Alder, Glenn and Doris Suarez. *Union Voices: Labor's Response to Crisis.* Albany: SUNY Press, 1993.

Aronowitz, Stanley. *From the Ashes of the Old: American Labor and America's Future.* Boston: Houghton Mifflin, 1998.

Becher, Bernd and Hilla Becher. *Industrial Façades.* Cambridge: MIT Press, 1995.

Benjamin, Walter. *The Arcades Project.* Translated by Howard Eiland and Kevin McLaughlin. Cambridge: Harvard U.P., 1999.

Bruno, Robert. "Everday Constructions of Culture and Class: The Case of Youngstown Steelworkers." *Labor History* 40: 2 (1999): 143–176.

——. *Steelworker Alley: How Class Works in Youngstown.* Ithaca: Cornell U.P., 1999.

Corn, David. "Dreams Gone to Rust: The Monongahela Valley Mourns for Steel." *Harper's Magazine.* September, 1986: 56–64.

Deaux, Kay and Joseph C. Ullman. *Women of Steel: Female Blue-Collar Workers in the Basic Steel Industry.* New York: Praeger, 1983.

Dickerson, Dennis C. *Out of the Crucible: Black Steelworkers in Western Pennsylvania, 1875–1980.* Albany: SUNY Press, 1986.

Feuchtmann, Thomas F. *Steeples and Stacks: Religion and Steel Crisis in Youngstown.* Cambridge: Cambridge U.P., 1989.

Galloway, Joseph L. "True Grit in a Steel Town." *U.S. News & World Report.* June 12, 1995: 30, 32.

Lynd, Staughton. "Youngstown Ohio: Rebuilding the Labor Movement from Below." In *Fire in the Hearth: The Radical Politics of Place in America.* Mike Davis, Steven Hiatt, Marie Kennedy, Susan Ruddick, and Michael Sprinker, editors. London: Verso, 1990.

Marquis, Christopher. "When the Fires Go Out: A steel town settles into decay." *The Progressive.* June, 1986: 23–25.

McIntyre, Richard. "Theories of Uneven Development and Social Change." *Rethinking Marxism* 5:3 (1992): 75–105.

Metzgar, Jack. "The Humbling of Steelworkers." *Socialist Review* 75/76 (May–August, 1984): 40–71.

Roediger, David. *The Wages of Whiteness: Race and the Making of the American Working Class.* London: Verso, 1991.

Rogivin, Milton and Michael Frisch. *Portraits in Steel.* Ithaca: Cornell U.P., 1993.

Schmiechen, Bruce, Lawrence Daressa, and Larry Adelman. "Steelworker Revival: Waking from the American Dream." *The Nation.* March 3, 1984 (v. 238): 241–44.

Terkel, Studs. *Working.* New York: Pantheon, 1972.

CAPITALIZATION

1.

Capitalize the first word
of every sentence, whether or not
it is a complete sentence.
Capitalize the first word of every line
of poetry. **I started work**
on an assembly line
at the huge Westinghouse plant
in East Pittsburgh when I was sixteen.
The work was dull and repetitive.
From 1954 to 1962,
Ronald Reagan served as host
of the television program, "G.E. Theater."
In some modern English poetry forms,
only the first word of the first line
is capitalized, and sometimes
even this is written lower-case.
Six times a year he acted in the dramas
(once starring in a two-part program
as an FBI agent who infiltrates
Communist-front organizations).
We tried to make the time go
by talking to each other.
Capitalize *father* and *mother*
when used in address, but do not
capitalize such nouns
when a possessive pronoun
is used with them.
The remainder of the year
Reagan toured G.E. factories,
speaking to employees and local civic groups on,
as he put it in his autobiography,
"the attempted takeover of the [electrical] industry
by Communists" and "the swiftly rising tide
of collectivism that threatens to inundate
what remains of our free economy."
Sometimes I would fantasize,
making believe I was somewhere other

than at that long bench
with the never-ending noise,
the whining of machines.

2.

During his eight years
on the old General Electric Theater,
Reagan enjoyed certain distinct
professional advantages.
Hundreds of women worked
at those benches. With prosperity,
more and more were added.
References for authoritative capitalization
of American and British names: *Who's Who,*
Who's Who in America,
Dictionary of National Biography,
Dictionary of American Biography.
But when the market crashed in 1929,
the benches were emptied almost overnight.
While the program's other performers
were at the mercy of the weekly dramatic material—
it was an anthology series—the star was not.
I don't know
how many were let go,
but my gosh, it was devastating.
He was no more responsible
for the quality of the shows
than for the quality of G.E.'s products.

3.

In spite of those tough times,
there was a feeling of solidarity.
If a family was put out of their house,
people would gather there to stop the eviction.
As the "host," he occupied a more defensible position.
It was Reagan who ended each show
with the famous slogan,
"Here at General Electric,
progress is our most important product."
When gas and electricity were shut off,
unemployed workers would go around
and turn them back on.
Do not capitalize the following
when they stand alone: judge, justice
Capitalize President
Capitalize Vice President
Capitalize Senator, Congressman
Capitalize Speaker
Capitalize Governor, Mayor, Cardinal
That "here" was located at some imaginary point
between General Electric itself and your living room.
But unlike more recent TV pitchmen,
such as Lee Iacocca and Frank Perdue,
Reagan was never burdened
with the pretense that he was himself
part of the actual production.
He never purported to know anything
about building cars, plucking chickens,
or designing light bulbs.
They fought for surplus food, then flour,
oleo and dry milk were distributed.
Capitalize all Government titles
when referring to definite persons
in high positions or to their positions,
and all titles of honor or nobility
when referring to specific persons.
On the contrary, our host was someone like us—

a typical consumer of the sponsor's products.

There were kidney beans and canned meat, too. Not gourmet, but it was something to eat.

4.

Before the crash of 1929,
I accepted things without question.
The evening classes at the Y
caused me to question, but I had no answers.
Bryn Mawr was the turning point.
The girls from the garment industry,
from Sweden and other places
talked of their unions
and how they worked.
That hit home.
Thousands of air traffic controllers
walked off the job at 7 a.m. yesterday,
snarling air traffic across the nation
and drawing an ultimatum from President Reagan,
who said his administration will fire any striking controller
who has not returned to work by 11 a.m. Wednesday.
Capitalize a title of preeminence
or distinction following the name of a person
or when used alone as a substitute for a name.
Ronald W. Reagan, fortieth President
of the United States; the President; the Chief
Executive; the Commander in Chief
We at Westinghouse had nothing to say
about our jobs, seniority, vacations,
pensions, and medical payments.
There was a company union,
but we had no real power.
In his morning briefing, Reagan made it clear
that the administration intends to make good
on its threat to prosecute controllers
who strike in violation of federal law.
Capitalize the words *department, bureau,*
service, station, office, agency, commission
and *board* if referring to a bureau
or executive department
of the u.s. Government
when the name is given.

**The need for workers
to band together
for the good of all
was the answer for me.
I believed it then,
and I believe it now.**

*Federal counteraction
included U.S. attorneys
in 11 cities
filing criminal complaints
in federal courts
against 22 PATCO officials
and local union strike leaders.*

5.

Capitalize *Federal* and *State Courts*
when used with a definite name.
Do not capitalize *city* and *county courts*.
When I came back home,
the idea of a union
of Westinghouse workers was strong.
u.s. *District Judge Harold H. Greene*
last night found the air traffic controllers union
and president Robert E. Poli
in contempt of a federal court order
prohibiting the strike
and gave union officials 24 hours
to get the controllers back to work
or pay a $250,000 fine.
Capitalize *Court* when meaning a judge
or judicial tribunal in direct personal reference
to such a judge or tribunal.
Evelyn, Helen, and I
heard there was to be a meeting
at Kidd's Hall in Turtle Creek
to discuss the possibility
of organizing at Westinghouse.
Almost lost in the conflict, which was developing
into a dramatic test of wills between the government
and what is regarded
as its most militant federal union,
was a singular bit of irony:
patco *was one of the few unions*
to break ranks with organized labor
and support Reagan
in the 1980 presidential race.
Capitalize the word *Cabinet*
when referring to the Cabinet
of the President of the United States.
In the White House Cabinet Room,
where Reagan met yesterday
with his advisers on the strike,

a portrait of Calvin Coolidge hangs.
Reagan and others approvingly mentioned
Coolidge's handling of the Boston police strike
during his administration, quoting his remark
at the time: "There is no right to strike
against the public any time, anywhere."
We went there,
and I was nominated recording secretary
of Local 601 of the United Electrical
and Radio Workers
of America.

6.

"The skies shall be silent."
The work of organizing went on.
So read the sign on the door of Local 204
of the Professional Air Traffic Controllers Organization
in Leesburg, where striking controllers milled about,
waiting to resume their picketing
for the afternoon shift
at the Washington Air Route
Traffic Control Center just outside town.
The executive board met weekly,
and applications trickled in.
William B. Simpson, president of the union,
suggested at a meeting
that I be put in charge of the office
on a full-time basis.
Spirits ran high among the strikers
in Leesburg yesterday, both in the union hall
and on the picket line.
They were calmly defiant of President Reagan's threat
to fire the strikers if they were not back on the job
Wednesday morning.
Usage varies as to the capitalization
of *administration.*
When referring to the political party in power
or when used with a name
to designate a Government board,
administration is usually capitalized.
It was felt that if someone was there,
workers would have a place
to come and talk.
It would give them the feeling
that the union was not temporary.
As 10 state troopers
and a dozen Loudoun County sheriff's deputies
stood by with two police dogs,
the picketers walked in an orderly circle.
Believe me, I did a lot

of soul searching before I agreed.
There were cries of "Scab!"
when some controllers drove by the picket line
to work the afternoon shift.
Picketers snapped their pictures
and recorded their names.
But I could remember my father
in the coal mines.
Capitalize the Republican Administration
Capitalize the Administration
Capitalize the Reagan Administration
"We want to know who's for us
and who's against us," said one controller
who wore a Polish "Solidarity" button.
He fought to build that union,
even with the coal and iron police there.
My mother, a woman of great courage,
said, "Take it, Margie."
And I did.

7.

As tensions grew yesterday
in the air traffic controllers mortal struggle
with the Reagan administration,
it was increasingly clear that the strike
has become a psychological touchstone
for frustrated employees in other federal unions,
and could set the tone
for government labor relations for some time.
Capitalize *Government* when used
synonymously with the U.S. Government
Before quitting, I talked
to the personnel manager, Johnny Schaffer.
I can remember going up to him—
I had more guts than brains—saying,
"I'd like a leave of absence."
The federal unions represent a vast array
of occupations, from nurses and clerks
to metal workers and machinists.
Do not capitalize *government* when referring
to that of a state in the United States
or that of any possession of the United States.
Further, the government is in effect a "right-to-work" state
in which workers can't be compelled to join and pay dues.
When he asked me why, I told him the truth,
that we were opening up a union office.
Capitalize *commonwealth,*
confederation, powers, union, etc.,
if used with proper names or as proper adjectives.
Capitalize Union of Soviet Socialist Republics
He said, "You know we can't
give you a leave of absence for that.
It just isn't our policy.
Capitalize *Constitution*
Also *act, bill, code, law, report,* and *treaty*
with a name or number to designate
a particular document are capitalized.
And you know you're never going to succeed.

They've tried it before."
Years ago there had been a strike
at Westinghouse that was broken.
There was bloodshed.
Capitalize Smith Act

8.

The organization of the CIO,
the sit-downs, added to
the electricity of the moment.
You could sense it in the air.
If FAA were operating in the private sector
they would have faced charges
of failure to bargain in good faith
from the National Labor Relations Board.
Capitalize *nation* and *republic*
when used as synonyms
for the United States
Capitalize *national*
when preceding a capitalized word.
Instead they enjoy the full force
of federal legal machinery
and the judicial system
in attempting to stifle
the legitimate demands of PATCO
and the workers it represents.
Capitalize *state*
when used with a name
or when used in place of the name,
but lower-case when used
as a general term.
Finally, at Westinghouse,
UE Local 601
was able to get recognition.
It was very exciting.
Note the usage of capitalization
in the following examples:
state prison
State's attorney
state's evidence
Southern states
a foreign state

9.

"I think [Reagan] forced the strike
so he could show big business that he can and will
beat up on union workers," said Thomas McNut,
president of UFCW Local 400 in Baltimore.
But as the benefits we gained grew,
those of us in the forefront
became targets of red-baiting.
Capitalize the names of organized bodies
and their adherents.
Capitalize Republicans, Shriners
Capitalize Socialists, Elks
They red-baited me.
They red-baited Charlie Newell
and those who represented
the left in our union.
"I get a strange feeling that our democracy
is seriously being challenged when
the administration says, 'Either you work
or we'll destroy you economically,'"
said David Wilson, director-elect
of District 8 of the United Steelworkers.
The only thing they had to throw at us
was that we were "Communists"
or that we were being led around
by the nose by Communists.
Usage differs as to the capitalization
of the word *party.*
the Communist Party
or the Communist party
The "red" label—
people were frightened by it.
From then on,
I don't think there was ever a time
when we weren't vilified by the press.
"Historically, when Americans
have been confronted with laws
that are unfair and unjust,

they have ignored them," Thomas Bradley,
president of the Maryland
and District AFL-CIO said.
"That's how the labor movement began."
It caused a real division in the union.
That's just what the company wanted.
You could not see
the hand of the company openly,
but somehow you knew
it was a hidden force.

10.

Then all the stops were pulled out
in the smear campaign
against the UE
when a rival organization, the IUE,
was established nationally.
The Reagan administration started firing
striking air traffic controllers yesterday
and federal judges put five of their number
behind bars, but the union appeared
to be holding firm
in the third day of its nationwide strike.
Do not capitalize clubs, associations,
institutions, orders, colleges, and the like
when used alone, unless
they have the value of a proper noun.
He belonged to a carpenters' union.
Churches preached
and the press editorialized.
Father Rice had organized
the Association of Catholic Trade Unionists.
They got into red-baiting, too.
While the notices were being put in the mail,
striking controllers and their families
met across the nation for rallies
sometimes interrupted by federal marshals
seeking to serve union leaders and members
with court orders against the strike.
You had Congressman McDowell
of the *Wilkinsburg Gazette*,
a little tabloid that carried articles,
shouting "Red!" every week.
Capitalize points of the compass when
they designate geographical parts of the country.
The South has increased its manufactures.

11.

It was in that atmosphere
that an election was ordered
to determine who represented
the workers at Westinghouse.
Lewis, under orders from President Reagan,
has refused to negotiate with the union
during the illegal strike.
Lewis said yesterday
that the administration is more concerned
about "how we rebuild the system"
once the thousands of expected
controller terminations take effect.
The UE and the IUE were on the ballot.
The hysteria mounted.
The Un-American Activities Committee
was going full blast against the UE.
Capitalize all proper names
denoting political divisions.
Capitalize the Republic (United States)
Capitalize the Papal States, Ward Ten
Capitalize Orange County
Capitalize *church*
Capitalize *cathedral, synagogue,*
temple, and *chapel*
when used with a name
Capitalize all names for the Bible
"Planes come too close and you get scared
and by the next day you forget it," he said.
"But that fright is cumulative, it builds
and pretty soon you're scared to go to work."
Even Hubert Humphrey,
the great "liberal," sent a message
to workers at Westinghouse:
If you vote for the UE,
the question of national security
comes into play, and we don't know
whether the company will get
any more government contracts.

12.

A spokesman for the Department of Justice,
Arthur Brill, said the conflict marked
one of the first times the Government
had brought criminal charges
against striking Government employees.
But Westinghouse succeeded in doing
what they had to do: They eliminated
the militant core of the union.
Capitalize *Heaven* when referring
to the Deity, and *Paradise*
and *Heaven* only when referring
to the hereafter; also *Hades*, but not *hell*.
He said, too, that it apparently
was the first time Government workers
had ever struck in such vast numbers
and the first time dismissal notices
had been sent out at anything
like the current level.
But: Sharecropping, no heaven
for the tenant,
was no paradise for the farmer.
The company really won that fight.
When they attacked the UE,
they broke up a good, honest union.
I think Father Rice is a little ashamed
of the role he played then.
Capitalize the *Pope*, or the *Popes*, always;
also *Holy Father, Pontiff*, and *Holiness*
Capitalize *Devil*, the *Evil One*, the *Adversary*
President Reagan has said there would be
"no amnesty" allowing a controller
to retain his job if, without a valid reason
such as sickness, he had missed
the deadline for returning to work.
Mr. Lewis said the only reason
many more notices had not gone out today
was "a matter of mechanics."

Capitalize the *Father of Lies*
Capitalize *Beelzebub*
Do not capitalize
when used in general sense
or as an expletive.

13.

It was terrible even after the elections.
My God, it was terrible.
He was asked in the Oval Office whether,
as onetime head of the Screen Actors Guild,
he felt "any pangs about firing" workers.
The fear was so thick
you could cut it with a knife.
My family was continually victimized.
Mr. Reagan replied: "Oh you bet.
Anyone who went through the Great Depression
thinks that is the worst thing that can happen
to anyone. I do feel badly. I take no joy in this.
There just is no other choice."
Capitalize all names of holy days and holidays.
Capitalize Christmas, Easter
Capitalize Labor Day
My sister Evelyn had worked at Westinghouse
for more than twenty-five years.
One day, a United States marshal
came right up to her place of work.
In front of her shopmates,
they took her down for questioning.
The FBI went to Evelyn's home.
My sister Ella was hounded
from one job to another.
The decision whether to arrest
a particular employee, they agreed,
depended on the amount of evidence
gathered by the FBI
and on discretion
of local United States attorneys.
Capitalize the first word
of each item in an outline:
1. Attracting attention
2. Creating desire
3. Convincing the mind
4. Stimulating action

And the FBI had their eye on me, too.
They checked on my activities
with my neighbors, who later told me.
My nieces and nephews of school age
were pointed at by other children.
Talk about a police state—
we knew what that meant.

14.

President Reagan has done more
than defeat America's
striking air traffic controllers.
He has also unleashed
a twin-pronged legal offensive
to punish them with the sack
and the destruction of their union.
McCarthy called hearings
in Washington, where people
from Westinghouse were to testify.
Victory alone would have been prize enough
for democratic leaders elsewhere,
who rarely expect to win
disruptive nationwide strikes these days
and are usually relieved to settle
for some face-saving (and expensive) compromise.
But there are peculiarly American reasons
why Mr. Reagan can win
without magnanimity:
Do not capitalize the first word
of an indirect question or statement:
He asked what was the meaning
of the party's steady growth in power.
no other western leader
currently enjoys his domestic popularity
and no other western labour movement
is in such a sorry state
as the American Federation of Labour-
Congress of Industrial Organisations.
Evelyn had gotten a telegram
that she was to appear.
Well, it so happened
that she had very high blood pressure.
We worried that she could have a stroke.
Our family doctor had her admitted
to a hospital. Being hospitalized
excused her from the hearings,

but she was fired by the company
as a poor "security risk" anyhow,
without any supportive evidence.
And this after twenty-five years of service.
Such hammer-blows raining down
on one of their number
might have been expected to provoke
sympathetic action
from other members of the labour movement.
No doubt in most west European countries
it would. But the AFL-CIO,
whose executive was meeting in Chicago
on August 3rd when the strike started,
has hardly raised a finger to help,
bar a token appearance
by the federation's president,
Mr. Lane Kirkland,
on the picket line.

15.

Do not capitalize a parenthetical statement
that occurs in the middle of a sentence.
If the machinists (who service aircraft)
or the pilots had shown solidarity
with the controllers then Mr. Reagan
would not have had things all his own way.
Instead, he could have been faced
with the shutdown of all the country's airports.
The planes (all of them now out of date)
were grounded. *It is symptomatic*
of the current state of the American labour movement,
however, that the only sympathetic action
came from two foreign unions
(the Canadian and Portuguese controllers).
My husband, Joe, died in 1953.
I sold the house and took a job
at Putney School in Vermont.
My daughter, Cathy, was only three.
The immediate impact of the denouement
of the controllers' strike has been
to enhance Mr. Reagan's prestige:
shooting down a union
and two Libyan jets
has worked wonders for a president
who was already riding high in public esteem.
Capitalize the names and synonyms
for flags of nations: the Star-Spangled Banner,
Old Glory, the National Emblem, the Union Jack.
I realized that institution
was no home life for a little kid.
We left there after one term
and came back here and bought a farm.
We had a thousand hens and an egg route.
I worked so hard and didn't make anything.
But I had a home for my little girl and me.
The practical effect will be to stiffen
the resolve of mayors and governors faced with

their own rebellious public employees.
The long-term implication is that
the controllers' defeat could hasten
America's drift towards
an almost union-free society.

16.

*Former controllers are driving cabs
in Lansing, Mich., selling bathroom fixtures
in Long Beach, Calif., hanging wallpaper
in Atlanta, pipefitting in Drexel Hill, Pa.,
baking in Honolulu, roughnecking
in the oilfields of Oklahoma,
substitute teaching in Hot Springs, Ark.,
selling cars in Detroit
and underwriting life insurance in Baltimore.*
**When I peddled eggs in East Pittsburgh,
I'd meet up with many people
who worked at Westinghouse.
They greeted me like an old and trusted friend.
They'd say, "Margaret, if you tell us
those eggs are fresh, we know they're fresh."
I thought: It's good to have
that kind of reputation. It's good
to be able to look people in the face,
to shake a worker's hand
with no need to apologize.**
Capitalize both parts of a hyphenated word
if each part is ordinarily capitalized:
Anglo-American attitude
Scotch-Irish ancestry
anti-American

17.

Any doubt remaining as to
the Reagan Administration's attitude
toward those who dared to defy it
was erased in March 1982.
A detailed questionnaire
from the Justice Department
arrived at the residence
of each former employee.
One time I was organizing the union.
Next I was selling eggs.
How did that happen?
The cover sheet stated the interrogatories
were for the "convenience" of those appellants
"who do not have counsel."
It also demanded that the interrogatories
"shall be answered under oath."
Therefore the appellant was required
to swear before a notary public
that his answers were complete.
I think it happened
because the left-wing movement
contributed so much
to the strength of the union.
That strength had to be dissipated.
A list of words and expressions
showing their generally accepted capitalization
follows. Note that some words
derived from proper nouns
have developed a special meaning;
these words are no longer capitalized.
American history
bologna sausage
boycott
English literature
poor whites
puritanical ethics
russian dressing

Russian olive
Statement No. 2
un-American
The phrasing of the first question
was particularly significant:
"Are you now, or have you ever been
a member of PATCO?"
Get rid of it. Get it out of here.
If the left could be isolated
out in the country somewhere,
selling eggs,
would there be any reason
to worry?
Would there?

WORKS CITED

"Air Controllers Turn to Wide Variety of Jobs." *New York Times*. October 18, 1981: A24.

Barron, James. "On Picket Line, Words of Both Unity and Fear." *The Washington Post*. August 6, 1981: D21.

Brown, Warren. "u.s. Begins Firing Striking Air Controllers; Five Jailed." *The Washington Post*. August 6, 1981: A1.

Brown, Warren and Laura A. Kiernan. "Reagan Threatens to Fire Striking Controllers." *The Washington Post*. August 4, 1981: A1.

Hockstader, Lee. "Spirits Run High Among Controllers." *The Washington Post*. August 4, 1981: A6.

Matthews, Christopher J. "Your Host, Ronald Reagan: From g.e. Theater to the Desk in the Oval Office." *New Republic*. March 26, 1984: 15–18.

Sager, Mike and Suzanne Spring. "Union Leaders Support PATCO Walkout." *The Washington Post*. August 6, 1981: A8.

Sawyer, Kathy. "This Strike is a Blip on the Federal Labor Screen." *The Washington Post*. August 6, 1981: A27.

Schatz, Ronald W. *The Electrical Workers: A History of Labor at General Electric and Westinghouse, 1923–1960*. Urbana: University of Illinois Press, 1983.

Schultz, Bud and Ruth Schultz. *The Price of Dissent: Testimonies to Political Repression in America*. Berkeley: University of California Press, 2001.

Shertzer, Margaret. *The Elements of Grammar*. New York: Collier Books, 1986.

Shostak, Arthur B. and David Skocik. *The Air Controllers' Controversy: Lessons from the PATCO Strike*. New York: Human Sciences Press, 1986.

"Solidarity is not a word American unions know." *The Economist*. August 29, 1981: 27.

Witkin, Richard. "u.s. Begins Sending Dismissals to Controllers and Jails Five." *New York Times*. August 6, 1981: A1.

JUNE 19, 1982

1.

*There has been some controversy about the history of the word **unemployment,** since G. M. Young said that 'unemployment was beyond the scope of any idea which early Victorian reformers had at their command, largely because they had no word for it . . . I have not observed it earlier than the sixties'. (*Victorian England, *27; 1936).*

I often take a drink or two to get started. I drink when ever I have a chance. I drink to forget my troubles. I find that I need a drink in order to relax. I drink to ease the pain. I have good reasons for getting drunk.

*

Louisville slugger
"little motherfuckers"

unemployed structurally
Capitalized racially

profit margins
marginalized

people *polis*
parole

destabilized
democratic spaces

closed foreclosed
nation

states
reiterates

bleached
hate speech

2.

This was challenged by E. P. Thompson: 'unemployed, the unemployed, *and (less frequently)* unemployment *are all to be found in trade union and Radical or Owenite writings of the 1820s and 1830s: the inhibitions of "Early Victorian reformers" must be explained in some other way.'* (The Making of the English Working Class, *776n; 1963).*

I get angry easily. I feel like swearing all the time. At times, I feel like smashing things. At times, I feel like picking a fist fight with someone.

*

Fancy Pants
Topless Dance

industrial dreams
kept alive by machines

what Cultures us
replaces us

palatial
palaces

plantations
defense plants

Over fifty-five
billion served

enveloped the world
defeated the Reds

space Race
can never erase

Thrift stores
depopulate

3.

Certainly Thompson is right, but the history is complicated. **Unemployed** *is much older. It was first used of something not being put to use, from C16, but was applied to people from C17, as in Milton's 'rove idle unimploid' (1667), where the sense is of not doing something rather than being out of work, and is clear in a modern sense from an example of 1677: 'in England and Wales a hundred thousand poor people unimployed'.*

People often disappoint me. I often think, "I wish I were a small child again." I often feel I am being neglected. I have a strong need for someone to love me. I often pity myself. People don't seem to understand me.

*

emptied of
discarded by

vacated vacant
discontent

unlikely pivotal history
off recently laid

economically and ailing
horribly unequally of

Tide All Cheer
blight flight

Lodge dislodged
two Chinatowns

"Don't call me a fucker,
I'm not a fucker."

sucker punching
ubiquitous Whiteness

4.

The developing sense is important, because it represents the specialization of productive effort to paid employment by another, which (cf. WORK, job, LABOUR) has been an important part of the history of capitalist production and wage-labour. In several related words this development can be traced.

I am having to take medication to calm my nerves. I find that I must take drugs in order to feel good. I am unable to sleep unless I take sleeping pills or powders. My friends often supply me with drugs that make me feel better.

*

smashed glass class
exhortation

"This land is my land"
or Angel Island

smashed glass class
assimilation

No Applications
Being Accepted Today

Japanese cars
scrapes in a bar

smashed glass class
after factories deportation

like Chrysler was drowning
like closing Lynch Road

"like the anvil fell"
swinging sledgehammers

5.

On the one hand INDUSTRY *(q.v.) developed from the sense of a general quality of diligent human effort to its modern sense of productive institution. On the other hand* **unemployed** *and* idle, *which were general terms for being unoccupied with anything at that time (though* idle *had the much wider original meaning, from oE, of empty and useless), developed their modern senses of being 'out of paid employment', or of being 'in employment but not working'.*

I have a strong desire to leave my home/family. I am unable to trust my spouse. Our family is constantly in the midst of quarrels. I feel hate toward members of my family whom I usually love.

*

abandonment's politics
institutional deceit

prevarication
post-Poletown

Clothed Caucasian male
Clothed Japanese [*sic*] male

Naked Black female
similarly pivotal history

private property
vends public views

parts depart *denouement*
assembly lines lied

structures of fleeing
manufacturing

Occident's
vast accident

6.

*Employ itself developed from a general sense – 'emploied in affaires' (1584) – to the sense of regular paid work: 'publick employ' (1709); 'in their employ' (1832). There were 'Secretaries and Employed Men' in Bacon (1625), and from C18 **employer** (originally usually imployer) had its modern sense; employé and the American employee followed in C19.*

I dislike having people about me. I find myself crossing the street to avoid meeting people I know. Whenever possible, I avoid being in a crowd. I avoid people when it is possible. I prefer to be alone most of the time.

*

her Black breasts
his Testosterone his

internal combustion
engines anomie

"We went to see
a baseball game.

But when people saw
Chinese sitting there

they kicked us
and cursed at us.

I never went back."
He never came home

Louisville slugger
"little motherfuckers"

Bear hug
year of the Dog

7.

Employ as a noun of condition is recorded from C17, and **employ** as an abstract social term can be found from C18. Both **employ** and **unemploy,** as nouns of condition acquiring a general and abstract social sense, can be found from lC18 and eC19; they pre-date their modern equivalents **employment** and **unemployment.** Thus all the necessary words were available by at latest lC18, and became common, in the new scale of the problem but also in the way that the problem was seen, as a social condition, from eC19.

I'm having difficulty in starting to do things. I seem to have given up. I've stopped trying because all that I do seems to end in failure. I feel as though I am paralyzed. It is as though I feel numb all over.

*

All Sexy Come
Nude Show See

service industries
basement laundries

". . . service them
either by giving them

a lap dance
or a hand job . . ."

unemployment: 17%
laid pink slips off

hunger emergency
human commodities

the dead bolts
the Master Locks

discounted rocks
the windows

8.

Employ *was from fw* employer, *F, from the passive form,* implicari, *L – involved in or attached to, rw* implicare, *L – enfold, involve (which also gave us* imply*). Its early sense was to apply something (C15) to someone (C16) to some purpose; both senses are still active. In the history of wage-labour this became, as we have seen, taking into paid work.*

I have a difficult time sleeping. I have a habit of biting my fingernails. I have nightmares every few nights. Almost every day something happens to frighten me. I often feel all wound up.

*

suture class structure
to racialized future

two autoworkers
White out of workers

location politics of
eye Color collar

singing "Don't it
make my brown eyes

blue" stripes White
stripping Starlene

urban impact detritus
suburban impact Gap

hooded sweatshirts sweatshops
Red-lined neighborhoods

the tired retired
and retreated

9.

The interaction with idle *is particularly interesting. The wide sense, in application to people, can be illustrated from c. 1450: 'To devocionne evre and Contemplacionne / Was sho gyven and nevre ydel.' But in an act of 1530-1 we find the characteristic 'to arest the sayde vacaboundes and ydell persones'.*

Most of the time I feel blue. I feel like giving up quickly when things go wrong. Things are so bad that I feel as though life is hardly worth living. I am often worried about possible dangers that I cannot control. I am often tempted to give up trying to solve my problems.

*

pushed the frame
named names

depression repression
the song the same remains

"Drive your Chevrolet
through the U.S.A.

America's the greatest
land of all."

stolen stereo types
discriminatory democracy

participatory
plutocracy

windows replaced
by the wind

begin
shattering

10.

*This has lasted long enough, but already in 1764 Burn observed: 'they are idle for want of such work as they are able to do' – a perception of **unemployment** in the modern sense.*

I believe that I am being plotted against. I tend to be on guard with people who are somewhat more friendly than I had expected. I find that I have lost my faith and trust in the future. I am troubled with the idea that people are watching me on the street. I do not trust certain members of my family. Someone has it in for me. I feel that it is certainly best to keep my mouth shut.

*

See Free Press
graffiti

what's the dirty
little secret

exposed overexposed
Caucasian cavities

"never was a racist"
just swung sledgehammers

Japanese cars
barroom brawls

scrawled abandonment
rented U-Hauls

to Phoenix Houston
maced malaise sprayed

comrade
or comprador

11.

*Clearly the modern (from lC18) sense of **unemployment** depends upon its separation from the associations of idle; it describes a social situation rather than a personal condition (idleness). There has been a steady ideological resistance to this necessary distinction; that is the point of Thompson's criticism not only of Young's history but of Young.*

Much of the time my head seems to hurt all over. I am bothered by pains over my heart or in my chest. My heart sometimes pounds as if it were coming out of my chest. I frequently notice my hands shaking when I try to do something.

*

Dragon Restaurant
Tiger Stadium

"Oriental gentleman"
brains on the street

Louisville slugger
"little motherfucker"

wrote his name
Vincent Chin

Lily's story
same Old Glory

unemployed structurally
Capitalized racially

White stars
Topless bars

Oh say
say you can see

12.

The resistance is still active, and in relation to the words is especially evident in the use of idle, *in news reporting, to describe workers laid off, locked out or on strike. With its strong moral implications,* idle *in this context must have ideological intentions or effects. 'Many thousands idle' sticks in the mind.*

I am sure I get a raw deal from life. I feel as though I am a condemned person. I seem to have very little control over what happens to me. I am being made to suffer for the actions of others. I feel as though I have been betrayed.

*

All that is solid
melts in the pot

moved South
emptied out

intolerant American dollar
torn blue collar

skull split shift blame
it's just a game

". . . swung the bat
as if a baseball player

swinging for a home run,
full contact . . ."

All that is solid stolen or sold
base bias bigotry gold

and bones are at the bottom
of the melting pot

WORKS CITED

Buss, Terry F. and F. Stevens Redburn. *Shutdown at Youngstown: Public Policy for Mass Unemployment.* Albany: SUNY Press, 1983.

Choy, Christine, and Renee Tajima. *Who Killed Vincent Chin?* New York: Filmmakers Library, 1988.

Williams, Raymond. *Keywords: A Vocabulary of Culture and Society* (Revised Edition). New York: Oxford University Press, 1983 (1976).

FRANCINE MICHALEK
DRIVES BREAD

NOTE: "Francine Michalek Drives Bread" is a fictional work. Resemblances to characters living and dead, fictional and non-fictional, are (just) coincidence. Textual samplings from speeches by the protagonist in Bertolt Brecht's *The Mother* and Mary Ann Landis's interview with Theresa Pavlocak (published in Thomas Dublin's compendium of oral history interviews, *When the Mines Closed: Stories of the Struggles in Hard Times*: Cornell U.P., 1998) provide historical underpinnings for this fictional tale.

act/one

Francine Michalek drives
        bread. Taystee
Bakery:

an occasion but not an option.
        So we went
home

to visit my mother. Francine,
        her mother, her
story,

her (driven) gestures. *I can't do*
        a thing to make it
any better.

Francine
        rises
to make it;

she drives through her
        morning
as she drives.

Somewhere
        Teamsters
like her.

My mother
        was all
alone

because the two boys
        were gone.
When inside her

truck is almost
            outside her
kitchen.

Not an option for her,
            but better?
What right

do I have, anyway, to eat
            here and live
in his room

and buy my clothes
            out of his
paycheck?

One was in Japan
            and Leyte. And
my brother

Frank was in
            Pensacola,
Florida.

Somewhere
            (other)
her brothers

got to go by driving,
            got there
by going

and were gone. Francine
            hears her
alarm clock,

wakes slowly
            to Loretta
Lynn.

Her co-workers (already)
      all night
awake

and baking
      at Taystee.
Nothing

helps. I see nothing
      to be
done.

act/two

So my mother
         lived
all alone

and we visited
         my mom.
Francine, her

father
         dead
already

(from Croatia, and her
         mother
was, too . . .

If Loretta Lynn's
         singing
if Francine's

coffee brews. *I'm afraid*
         I can't boil
any tea.

We haven't enough. With
         what there is
I couldn't make

decent tea. The pants Francine
         wears she puts
on next

to the toaster, reading
         the day
before's mail.

My husband
    said to her,
"Mom.

If you can get me
    a job
in a colliery,

we're going
    to move
back."

Mother Croatia brother
    Japan brother
Pensacola,

Florida. Francine,
    meanwhile,
with Eleanor

driving over
    to Taystee.
He was glad

to have the job,
    when he first
went to work.

It's true he wasn't
    paid much.
And in the past

year it's gotten smaller
    and smaller.
He said, "Maybe

when the war is over
    that job
won't last,

I'll be out of work
   again."
Her job

is the occasion of her
   rising,
yet away

from Taystee
   she drives.
It's where

she stays, nonetheless,
   and has,
for something

like twenty-nine years.
   Not rising
is not her option.

Then there's working
   here in
the house,

with machines that have
   to be hung outside
the window.

She said, "Do you
   mean it, Mike?"
He says, "Yeah."

In front of the window
   there has to be
a curtain hung.

Because you couldn't
   get a job
in the colliery

at one time; you
   had to know
somebody.

act/three

Francine Michalek risen
      and arriving;
not to is not for her

to choose. Otherwise
      Eleanor
leaves

the lights on. **We went
      back;
we were gone**

**about three weeks and
      the phone rang;
it's my mother.**

*It all depends upon
      what kind of a man
this gatekeeper is.*

*Whether he's a lazy
      or a careful one.
What I have to do*

*is to get a pass
      out of him.*
Working

all night's another
      Eleanor,
another

Francine, lifting and loading
      the trucks,
the bread,

and still there are
              others
who drive

the lifting and loading
              through
the morning.

She said, "Mike, you
              have a job
if you want

to come." So Francine
              sold it all
and they

moved, she remembered, as
              she pulled the
Taystee truck

out onto Luzerne Road.
              She took
to humming

that way. Hmm, hmmmmm.
              You're perfectly
right.

All I'm doing is keeping you.
              Without any
questioning at all,

he said, "We're going."
              We put the furniture
in the van

and moved in
              with my mother
and stayed

**until the brothers
       came home.**
Her first stop

is Piggly
       Wiggly.
She enters

(and leaves) through
       the loading
doors.

act/four

Something by Aunt Molly
      Jackson is
what she

catches herself humming
      at first.
Taystee

it says on one side of her
      jacket; and
on the other,

of course, Francine. *You see,*
      then. This table
belongs

to me, for instance. Now
      let me ask you
whether

I can't do just as I want
      with this table?
Can I chop it up

for kindling wood
      if I want?
Furniture,

Francine, the furniture
      Mike is
moving

into the Perpich family
      basement.
I only had one

daughter. When she
            was five
and a half,

she was going into
            first grade.
Her mother, she

remembers, was always
            awake
when she left

for Taystee. "We're short
            a dozen
loaves,"

he tells her. *What do you expect
            me to cook? Where
will the rent*

*come from? Tomorrow
            morning you
won't go to work.*

*How will things stand
            tomorrow night?*
"You only ordered

nine racks," she snaps
            back. *And what will
matters be*

next week? Back inside
            her truck
she's saying

"Fucking Assistant Managers;
            think they rule
this goddamn world."

She checks her rear-view
        mirror; nothing
in the parking lot

behind her. Yet she
        double-checks,
Francine, twice.

She has never caused
        an accident.
Her first day

of school, we were going
        into
church

with his body in the casket.
        Her first
day of school—

[my husband] got
        killed
in Coaldale

colliery. [We'd
        only been
back]

a couple of months,
        and he got
killed.

act/five

Mother as in Mother Courage;
    Mother as in
Mother Jones.

I went along to help
        demonstrate
for the workers' cause.

The people marching there
        were decent,
orderly people, who had

worked hard all their lives.
    It happened
on a Saturday

morning, and the first day
        of school
was Monday.

I was in Bright's buying
        her shoes
for the first

day of school. At the same
        time, earlier,
afterwards,

turning the Taystee wheel.
        Francine turning
something

over, recollecting Michael,
        recalling the truck,
driving

Francine
     forward
to the next

grocery chain. **He went**
     to work
that morning,

Saturday morning. Eleanor
     eating
in the commissary;

Francine, later, brown-bagging
     it, too. *There were*
also, of course,

some desperate people,
     driven to
extremes because

they had no jobs; also
     some hungry
people, too weak

to defend themselves.
     Her Taystee
AM radio,

the voice of someone
     always trying
to sell her

something. Francine, drive
     and hum.
I was down

buying shoes for her, when
     they came over
to me and told me

I'm wanted. *You must not*
            give it up.
Nothing

can happen to you . . . Give it
            here! I will take it.
All of this

must be changed. **They**
            never told me
why.

act / six

What is taught Francine
      is taught across
the world

unequally. Taut like
      a rope
and even more

like a rope can
      teach.
They put me

in the car. My mother
      lived on
Ridge Street.

Put me in a car and they
      stopped off at
my mom's home.

Every day Francine is driving
      from this
morning on.

Must it really be "Branch, nest,
      fish"? Because
we are old people

we have to learn the words
      we need
quickly! Long before

lunch, up until supper, braking
      and then slowly
moving

ahead. Yellow lights red lights
        green lights; yellow
lights green lights

red. *You're here to learn*
        reading and writing,
and that's

something you can *do here.*
        Yellow lights
red lights

green lights; yellow
        lights green
lights

red. *Reading, too,*
        is class struggle.
Took my daughter

in and came out
        without her.
Francine

Michalek drives bread;
        rising was
what drove her.

Teaching, taught or taut across
        the world
unequally;

taught or taut like her
        throat.
Red lights,

red, Francine . . . *you must put*
        your hand
down firmly;

otherwise it trembles, and
        nobody can read
your writing.

act/seven

They took me right down
      the hill, and
pulled up in front

of the hospital. The Piggly
      Wiggly, outside of
Union, is Francine's

last stop of the day.
      Outside Eleanor
smokes a Slim.

And humming, Francine to
      Francine.
I never dreamed

I would have to pass
      my last years
like this. **Before**

they took me in to see him,
      Doctor Steel
was the doctor

at that time, they took me
      into a little
room

and they told me exactly
      what's wrong
with him.

Her father was a preacher,
      miner, and
union organizer

who taught her to stand up
        for the rights
of common people.

She was writing tunes
        by age four,
walking

picket lines with her father
        at age five,
and by ten

she'd spent time in jail for her
        family's union beliefs.
They make sure

to let us know when our time is
        past. We have
nothing

to look forward to. Everything
        we've learned
belongs

to the past. **He told me**
        he wouldn't
live,

the two hips were crushed
        and one arm
was practically

mangled. *And our experience*
        means nothing.
And maybe

that's why Francine was
        humming
them songs.

act/eight

Aunt Molly Jackson
       married
at fourteen

and was working as a nurse
       -midwife
among

the local poor mountaineers
       shortly afterwards;
Francine

caught herself
       humming
her songs.

Her Taystee truck
       empty,
Francine,

waiting for Eleanor to be
       through.
They told me

it's only a matter
       of time.
Who

does the slaughtering?
       All
I remember,

I fainted. Her father
       and brother
were blinded

in mining accidents,
            Aunt Molly
Jackson.

**That I know. I could
            remember that.**
Her first

husband, her son, and
            another
brother

were killed
            working
in an industry

that barely paid them enough
            to survive, Aunt
Molly Jackson.

**When I came to, they
            took me
over to him.**

Oh God, he looked terrible.
            Her neighbors
were killed

by black lung, TB, and
            malnutrition, Aunt
Molly Jackson.

**So then they took him
            upstairs,
and he lived**

until midnight. During her
            lifetime seventy
thousand miners

were killed in the mines, and
            tens of thousands
of women and children

went on to live agonizing lives,
            Aunt Molly Jackson.
Then he died.

More than anything else,
            you have to start
with the idea

that where there's a worker
            all is not yet
lost.

Somewhere
            Teamsters
like her.

act/nine

"Kentucky Miner's Wife
        (Ragged Hungry
Blues)"

Eleanor asks Francine
        if she wants to stop
at Lou's.

(Take the needle from
        the record
if it skips,

skips to . . . *Just when
        the oppression*
gets strongest

is when people turn indifferent
        and pretend
they're happy

with all the dirt and meanness.
        After work, Francine,
Eleanor bowling

and beer. **He wasn't a coal**
        miner, he
was a loader.

The coal that the men had
        picked, what
-ever it was,

they had these little cars where
        they filled up
with coal.

"Over at Surdyk's," Eleanor says,
        "over at Surdyk's
you can get

one of those for one seventy-five."
        Francine, Taystee
on one side,

Francine, Francine on the other.
        "I got a couple
in the cupboard.

Got me a couple from there."
        They were going
with these

cars over the rails,
        [Francine lowers
her head]

they were going around
        the curve and
the fellow

that was driving
        the motor,
whatever

they called it, was going
        kind of fast.
Francine,

her eyes closed; Eleanor
        saying something
about some

-thing for twenty-nine cents
        less; Francine
". . . Ragged

Hungry . . ." and inhaling her
        Slim; Eleanor
asking, "Francine?"

act/ten

The Mother *attempts to combat*
        the indifference
shown

by the exploited toward their
        sufferings, even
in trivial

everyday events. **This was**
        Saturday
morning

about ten o'clock. Eleanor,
        Francine,
standing in

Lou's parking lot, standing on
        Lou's asphalt,
the rain making it

glisten a bit like coal. Maybe
        even humming
a bit, Loretta Lynn.

Of course, if your daddy doesn't
        want to go
on working,

he doesn't have to. But you need
        a coat.
At home

in the kitchen
        warming
a frozen

dinner; at home in the kitchen
        paging through
the news.

Except the Obituaries. **And ran**
        off the tracks,
and when the car

pinned him up against
        the timber, they said
he looked

like Christ on a cross, because
        it caught
the hips

and the two legs and an arm.
        She could remember
those old

television dials on the TV
        dinner boxes
when she first

started having them; she could
        remember
applying

for the driving job over there
        on Luzerne
Road.

Eleanor when they met was over
        at the commissary
reading the paper, too.

(Accept Obituaries.) Francine,
        she could see
she was moving

116

forward through her morning.
     Now go and tell
the snow

and the wind that right here is
     where they should
snow;

for here is where
     the coats
hang.

act/eleven

The television drones *All in*
    the Family;
Francine

watches them with Francine.
        Sometimes
at home

when she's humming, she'll
        catch her hands turning
an absent wheel.

It wasn't because of reason
        that I wept.
But when I stopped

weeping, that was not because of
        unreasonableness.
Francine

on her couch watching Archie
        in his chair;
the telephone

is not ringing in either where.
        Hmm-hmm-hmm,
hmmmmm-hmmmmm.

Till they pulled him out
        of there, it was
quite a while.

[He] lived like that until
        midnight.
Thinking

about not thinking about him
        any more. *What*
did you do

when God so ordained that you
        should be put out
onto the street?

Turning, like she does,
        the television
down;

Francine Michalek drives bread
        while Eleanor scrubs
industrial-size kitchens.

An occasion but not an option.
        Living, perhaps;
but living

very badly. Humming, Francine,
        humming . . .
"Mike,

oh Mike, are you still sleeping?"
        "Perhaps,
but sleeping

very badly." **He was**
        twenty-eight
years old.

act/twelve

I had a brother going for
        a priest
at the time.

With the same hands that drive
        with the same
hands that

brushing her hair. Francine.
        Fingers.
Rosaries.

With the same hands that. *No,*
        no, you have to
know

what's in these! It's our
        ignorance about
the spot we're in

that keeps us down.
        With the same
hands

that brushing her teeth. **He was**
        in Geneva,
Illinois,

about twenty-two miles north
        of Chicago. They
notified him,

and he came home.
        Under
the covers

until the morning is
        only
Francine.

I lived in the little home.
        Turning over
she reaches

with the same hands turning her
        alarm clock on.
Turning

again back over herself.
        Y-y-yesss,
but think of it:

all the world—(she shouts, so
        the frightened
Workers

clap their hands over her
        mouth) *is living*
in terrible darkness,

it's waited till now for
        you alone,
you

who could still be reached
        by reason.
Just think,

if you refuse! **I'd just**
        moved
into it,

my husband and I,
        up here
on East

**Kline Avenue on the five
hundred block.**

Francine

Michalek turning over;
          over
-turning.

act/thirteen

Francine, speaking, in her dream
        that is not
only *her* dream,

Francine, the Teamsters and
        everyone
like her.

Did anyone tell you that I have
        no money?
Having

next to nothing and next humming
        Aunt Molly Jackson.
My daughter

was going to the first day of school
        Monday or Tuesday.
They got him

out of there and [he] died at
        midnight, Her
daughter now lives

in Topeka; she got through school
        and became
a nurse.

Francine, awake, "Fucking Assistant
        Managers."
Francine

and Eleanor at the bar. Otherwise
        she leaves
the lights on.

After Lou's. **and that was it.**
　　　That was
the end

of my world. *During this Chorus,*
　　　The Mother
has laboriously

gotten up, dressed, taken her purse,
　　　and, uncertainly, but with
gathering strength,

crossed the room and gone out
　　　through the door.
Her daughter

had to have a mastectomy
　　　this past
November.

Francine, rising, staying on
　　　(this time
an option

for her); Francine, Teamsters
　　　Local 289's
new Secretary.

Eleanor told her not to be
　　　nobody's
notetaker,

but Aunt Molly Jackson was
　　　with her father
in that

county jail. Hmm-hmm-hmm,
　　　hmmmmm
-hmmmmm.

act/fourteen

They moved me out. They
       took me
down

to the seminary, to my brother
       the priest.
I was there

for two or three days. Furniture,
       Francine,
moving

that goddamn furniture again.
       Her hands
were not

on the U-Haul's steering wheel.
       I came home, and
they had me

moved out. At three o'clock in
       the morning, at four
fifteen

in the morning, at four forty-seven
       in the morning,
Francine Michalek.

No; we're turning it in so it won't
       end. Again Francine
at the toaster,

Francine into her pants; again
       the mail
and again

the day before. If Loretta Lynn's
          singing if
Francine's

coffee brews. The morning after
          Lou's. *Don't you*
hear

the bells? The bells ring for only
          two things;
a victory,

or a death. **My mother moved**
          everything
out of that little

home. I moved in with her,
          because she was
alone.

Eleanor, Francine, the patches on
          their jackets,
next to each other

in her car. "Are you coming to
          the meeting tonight?"
"If you're coming

to Lou's." *Alone,*
          there is nothing
you can do.

act/fifteen

Francine Michalek drives what is
     lifted and loaded;
bread is the occasion

and not the option. Turning over
     something, Francine,
Eleanor—

Overturning. Life like
     light
goes on.

My two brothers were
     in the service.
My dad

was dead at fifty. He died from
     a tumor
on his brain.

Life like light like life
     at Coaldale
mine.

Several years later, nevertheless,
     Francine married
another miner;

humming, just the way she does, her
     Aunt Molly Jackson;
and her Frank Michalek

died of a tumor in his brain. And
     the son that they had
together, also,

in the war in Vietnam. *You see,*
        there is still so much
that I have to do,

I, Pelagea Vlassova, the widow
        of a worker
and the mother

of a worker. Francine Michalek of
        Taystee Bakery;
it says so

here on this patch. And Eleanor
        and television
dinners,

and teaching what she's been
        taught.
Hmm,

hmmmmm, Aunt Molly Jackson.
        Mother
Courage

and Mother Jones. *No; when*
        I am tired, then
I'll give it to you

and you'll carry it. **So, I moved**
        in with Mom,
and that's where I stayed.

She took care of my
        daughter,
and I worked—

HOYT LAKES / SHUT DOWN

"It's important to note that this is not a people issue."

—RICHARD HIPPLE, LTV STEEL PRESIDENT

MAY 24, 2000

05.25.2000

"The shutdown will mark the first closing of one of the Iron Range's behemoth taconite plants since the 1980s, when a brutal shakeout closed two of eight mines and cut employment in the industry from 16,000 to 6,000."

My stomach dropped to the floor. It was like my stomach was hit by a 10-ton brick. We knew for the last few years that things weren't the best, but we never expected this. It's just unbelievable.

The factory of my father [reduced to rubble]. Factory [after factory (shut down)]. Seventeen stories. The blast furnace of my grandfather. The slaughterhouse across from the railroad [terminal] where my father's aunt used to work. Seventeen stories, and every single window shattered [shut up].

*

workers / words / worth / [repeating]

Iron : 21

05.25.2000

My neighbor across the street lived through the General Motors shutdown; the son (a bricklayer) of my next-door neighbor (a bricklayer) shot himself in the head.

It's like getting kicked out of your house . . . In my position [the speaker lost his leg in an accident at the mine a year ago] **I don't know what's going to happen now. I think the way it came down was totally wrong. In the 1980s it was due to the economy throughout the u.s. Now the economy is strong. I hope it's not politics. I hope Cleveland-Cliffs** [ltv] **is not pulling a fast one on us. Is there any glimmer of hope? I don't know. Everybody is usually talking. They're quiet . . . It's like everybody's been shot through the heart.**

"Jim Gorski, a millwright in his 31st year and the union recording secretary, said, 'I think this is going to be devastating not only to the young employees but to the old ones. I don't know how you rebound from losing 1,400 jobs.'"

*

"the American custom" = "the American customer"

Tower : 40

05.25.2000

In a nutshell, this is the most devastating thing to ever happen to this town. It's going to affect everybody. It's scary. It's very scary. We've had hard times before and survived, but this time, I just don't know . . . Apparently, our best quality isn't good enough for their blast furnace.

"The mine, which once employed more than 3,000 people, is the town of about 2,400's largest employer; the next largest business employs 42 people . . . Gov. Jesse Ventura said the state will do whatever is possible to help with the transition. 'Nobody likes to see companies close down and leave, but that's the negative part of doing business,' Ventura said."

Relocation [talks] at the dinner table. Windsor (Canadian). Shut up get ready to leave [for Asheville (North Carolina)]. Railroads steelworkers Westinghouse department store clerks cashiers Rosie the Riveters restaurant cooks. At least Genny Cream Ales came cheap.

*

Main Street — It Can't Happen Here

06.04.2000

He called me right away at work, and I was like: 'Shut up, Dave.'
I thought he was kidding. When you grow up around it and it's
supported your family, you assume that's what you are going to do,
too. I took it for granted that LTV would be there for my whole
career. I was sick to my stomach.

Discontinue normal program. Broadcast this announcement: "This is a test . . ."
Emergency [enclosures] cover [over] every [window] frame. Transmit attention
signal [for 20 to 25 seconds (see Sections 73.906 and 73.940 of the Rules)].
Broadcast announcement: "This is a test of the Emergency Broadcast System . . .
If this had been an actual emergency . . ."

"He said his family can't survive on an $8- or $9-an-hour job. He takes
home about $900 every two weeks and Lisa works part-time at Festival
Foods in Virginia . . . He ruptured a disk after a huge pipe rolled back
on him last year in the mine. He endures surges of back pain that can
make normal movements excruciating. Doctors expect them to get
worse and more frequent as he gets older."

*

ore / pits / fill / with / water

Gilbert : 131

08.20.2000

Other factors? Other factories? The junkyard across the street we could see from our [picture] window: one frame where broken got rusted got ingrained.

"This is not the life that Lisa Lislegard imagined ... One day there were rumors that LTV was bankrupt, the next day word was that a Japanese firm bought the mine. Then there were rumors that massive layoffs would begin this winter. Others said the mine would be open longer than earlier believed."

It's just so hard to know what's right. It's so hard because we aren't there. We don't know what's going on. There is just so much we don't know and so many things being said around town. I know we'll survive. Even if we have to live on hot dogs.

*

ground / rent / asunder

Biwabik : 51

10.08.2000

Used to play, my Uncle Ray kept repeating, we used to play in that dump behind Rejtan Street. Rats swimming around. Industrial [chemical] waste. Was so sick missed so many days I had to repeat first grade. And then they build houses over there?

The biggest thing is that it's going to have a trickle-down effect. It will affect everyone, from grocery stores to gas stations. It affects everybody up here. But it's happened before and we made it through it. We're fighters up here. You make it through those lean years and you go on.

"And already the effects of the impending shutdown are beginning to creep into the Range economy. Some vendors are starting to shed jobs, some people have begun to curb their spending and pay off debt, while some retailers are starting to feel a pinch, too. The ripple effect of the closure is projected to impact an additional 1,400 workers who are not employed by LTV."

*

what / disappears / in the distance / with / who

Ely : 54

11.19.2000–12.05.2000

The department store my mother sold coats took customer complaints stood on her feet was a cashier at; my father sold liquor stood when Westinghouse closed sold lottery tickets at a register worked at Radio Shack® was a cashier at.

"WAL-MART STARTS HIRING PROCESS: 'With more part-time employees, I can hire more,' explained Westenfield. 'If we get more people wanting full-time, we can't hire as many.'"

There seem to be more opportunities in the Hibbing area than the east end of the Range, noted Debevec, while pointing to the soon-to-be-open Wal-Mart. There is opportunity on the Iron Range. But change is hard, very hard to accept and handle. These people don't want change and don't want to sell themselves, but they are going to have to. It's just the tip of the iceberg.

*

<http://www.youareworthmore.org>

Hibbing : 20

12.07.2000–01.04.2001

"National Steel's former general manager, his wife and two consultants pleaded guilty in u.s. District Court [in Duluth] Wednesday to a scheme involving more the $240,000 in kickbacks, misappropriations and insurance fraud."

It sucks. It sucks. It sucks. But it's the same old story. You could see it coming for the last 10 years . . . They've already kicked you down to the ground, and now they keep kicking you in the head. I just want it to be over. It's devastating.

Strip mines frame strip malls "gains" as Capital claims its Local. The door [historical], the sometimes [seeming] impenetrable wall. But Luddites broke frames, hundreds of them. And the Range was once Wobbly, too.

*

Wal-Mart / wages / u.s.[w.]a. / away

Aurora : 262

01.06.2001–01.19.2001

"NATIONAL STEEL TO LAY OFF IO WORKERS"
"EVTAC NEXT MINE TO CLOSE?"
"HIBTAC WILL CLOSE FOR IO WEEKS"

One brick [broke (frames)] the remains of my father's factory. Ten less ten weeks less next [mine] to close. The background [under (ground)], the economic [limits (of)]. One miner one thousand four hundred miners minus miners minus plus. What broke [one brick] one miner one bricklayer what broke one worker down. Broken [under (ground)].

The plant was usually blowing smoke out of it. Today, there was nothing . . . We don't want to be here. It's embarrassing. We went through this in the early '80s. I remember standing in the cheese line. For us, it's a matter of life or death on the Iron Range. We don't want to see what happened in the early '80s happen again . . . Please help us. This is an economic tornado.

*

no tres- / no trees // -passing / leaves

Embarrass : 85

"We're all working together; that's the secret. And we'll lower the cost of living for everyone, not just in America, but we'll give the world an opportunity to see what it's like to save and have a better lifestyle, a better life for all. We're proud of what we've accomplished; we've just begun." —Sam Walton (1918–1992)

Not everyone was as enthused about the store's opening. Members of United Food & Commercial Workers Union Local No. 1116 picketed the entrances to the store. "Wal-Mart brings sub-standard wages and benefits to the area," Union representatives said in a statement.

*

"Windows® is shutting down . . ."

Babbitt : 55

05.06.2001–06.03.2001

It's been a crazy time around here. There's a lot of uncertainty and fear . . . I've heard the statement today that it's a nice day for a funeral. I think the statement pretty well sums up how people feel. It's kind of a sad occasion to see a place shut down where you worked for 36 years.

"[David] Lislegard has come to embody the plight of young miners suffering the wrath of a grim taconite industry. He and his young family are adjusting to life without LTV. The third-generation miner was at the beginning of what he thought would be a lifelong career at LTV when the mine shut down. Lislegard turned to union activity after LTV officials announced the closing. He became more involved in union committees, trying to ensure benefits for the unemployed miners. But he doesn't see mining in his future."

Paid bills paid dues shut stopped unpaid. Like storefronts the bus passed on my way to the unemployment office. Shut[down] trust, "in God we *rust," tell me who the fuck are "U.S." The smile plastic and purchased, community disembarked in the window.

*

stores / stories // tore out / [h]ours // as ore

Eveleth : 117

02.23.2002

"In December, after LTV stopped making steel, a U.S. bankruptcy judge approved a plan that allows the corporation to stop paying health-insurance premiums and supplemental unemployment pay at the end of February for laid-off workers, and in June for retirees."

LTV is pulling an Enron. They're reorganizing on the backs of the people who built the company. If they take over, I won't get a pension until I'm 62, and then it will be only about $400. I'm a veteran who served in Vietnam for a year and in the Persian Gulf for five months. Now, the government is going to help me—right out onto the street.

shhh . . . Shutter. shhh . . . shhh . . . shutter Shutter. shhh . . . Capital recovered. shhh . . . shhh . . . Shutter. shhh . . . shhh . . . shutter Shutter. shhh . . . Capital recovered. shhh . . . shh . . . shut. shh . . . up. shh . . . utter. shh . . . out. shhh . . . "This is not a people issue." shh . . . shhh . . . "This is [shhh . . .] a test . . ."

*

how // close // how // [*will*] // a -Rose

Hoyt Lakes : 212

WORKS CITED

Bloomquist, Lee. "Closing Hoyt Lakes, Minn.: Taconite Mine Leaves Former Workers Uncertain." *Duluth News-Tribune.* January 6, 2001: 1A.

———. "Deep Impact: Mine Closure Starts Ripple Effect." *Duluth News-Tribune.* October 8, 2000: 1A.

———. "Era Ends as Last Train Leaves Hoyt Lakes Taconite Plant." *Duluth News-Tribune.* June 23, 2001: 3C.

———. "LTV to Close in February." *Duluth News-Tribune.* December 7, 2000: 1A.

———. "Steel Company Layoffs: First Round Hits 30 Workers." *Duluth News-Tribune.* August 27, 2000: 1A.

Goerdt, Janna. "Last Shift to be Worked on Saturday." *Mesabi Daily News.* January 4, 2001: 1A, 10A.

Grinsteinner, Kelly. "Finding Jobs for LTV Workers No Simple Task." *The Daily Tribune* (Hibbing). November 19, 2000: 1A, 10A.

Helgeson, Baird. "Life After LTV." *Duluth News-Tribune.* September 24, 2000: 1A.

———. "LTV Shutdown: The Wives' Story." *Duluth News-Tribune.* August 20, 2000: 1A.

———. "Shutdown Weighs Heavily on Employees." *Duluth News-Tribune.* December 7, 2000: 1A.

———. "The Tale of Two Families." *Duluth News-Tribune.* June 4, 2002: 1A.

"Local Wal-Mart Opening Tomorrow." *The Daily Tribune.* January 27, 2001: 1B, 3B.

Lohn, Martiga. "LTV Miners Fight for Economic Life." *Duluth News-Tribune.* January 19, 2001: 1A.

"Mine Closing Rocks Range." *The Daily Tribune.* May 25, 2000: 1A, 16A.

"Plant Closing Hits Hard on Range: Taconite Mine is Old, Inefficient, LTV Says." *St. Paul Pioneer Press.* May 25, 2000: 1A.

Oakes, Larry. "Ex-LTV Workers Feeling Financial Pinch." *Star Tribune* (Minneapolis). February 23, 2002: 1B.

Oakes, Larry and Pat Doyle. "The End Comes Early in Mining Community." *Star Tribune.* January 4, 2001: 1B.

Swanson, Gwen. "Wal-Mart Starts Hiring Process." *The Daily Tribune.* December 5, 2000: 1A.

———. "Wal-Mart Superstore Opens." *The Daily Tribune.* February 28, 2001: 1A, 12A.

Tyssen, Linda. "Union Reacts to Shock." *Mesabi Daily News.* May 25, 2000: A1, 10.

"Wal-Mart: Helping People Make a Difference." *The Daily Tribune.* January 27, 2001: 2B.

AFTERWORD

AFTERWORD

by Amiri Baraka

CLASS REUNION

In the u.s., one of the principal problems with organizing the Revolutionary Democratic upsurge and certainly the Socialist Revolution that it prefaces is that in too many ways, the u.s. working class is not yet a "class for itself." Or I shd say, perhaps, it has approached that true self consciousness as in the '30s, Depression times, or as an undergirding activity of the Black mass's '60s upsurge, camouflaged into division by "race," and the invisibility of the white sector, as well the u.s. left's crude and subtle lack of understanding, passing over to social chauvinism of the Afro-American national question.

The social democratic opportunism of the left also distorts their perception and use of Culture in the struggle. Allowing the bourgeoisie to dominate the arts and socialize cultural workers and the people by not offering an alternative to the imperialist superstructure! All but disarming the arts as frivolous or marginalizing it, so that the most anti-imperialist writing, painting, cultural analysis is squashed out of sight in various obscure journals.

So the most visible, aggressively anti-imperialist art in the u.s., certainly, is the poetry & rap, largely by young Afro-American and Latinos, male & female, tho there is an emergence of some Asian and young white poets whose work is impressive in that tendency. The rappers are configured in the same ethnic presence. But to eyeball youngish white anti-imperialist, working class, left poets is still not usual. The main reason is that the class socialization & persona of "white people" is generally more magnetized to the pretended facsimile art of the social view that pitches seduction from inside the fake reality of America the Big Dog, so high and mighty that any focus on actuality seems grim and overstated. Or hysterical.

Nowak relies on his life as a person, not the addictive mist doping one into seeing themselves as a swollen category of intellectual whore, the literary, academic, blankness of the American "aesthetic." Though it is no longer limited to white folks alone, the journals, publishing & program cults, "'black' literary journals" such as there are, flaunt such gutted whorishness ubiquitously, pushing the fragmented minds of what the big dogs ate! The whore, or at least, unconscious body, can now be fitted for most Americans, since the "triumph" of the civil rights movement and the pretended "raising of all nations" has been rendered as real as nature, tho it is a lie!

So Nowak enters, socialized in a contemporary forwarding, advance, recall, re-assertion of the life, the sticks and stones: a child of immigrants, and with the sturdy underpinning of class (as life distinction), class alienation, and brings it back, humming. And sleek with seeing and hearing!

We get a sharp eye, a literary & philosophical broadening of what used to be labeled "working class poetry," scientifically, yes, deepened with a hard but contemporary lyric, and narrative. Hard image. Latering the academic construct, a fresher panorama of the more sophisticatedly excluded. The secret of u.s. class disconnection . . . pervasive use of race (&c) to make space between the different sectors of the class.

And these "past the past in the rust belt" Youngstown, the closing of the Youngstown steel mills. Grandfather a steel worker, Grandmother a Teamster, Bethlehem, Buffalo. Father, a union vp at Westinghouse, in that other "futha" non-ghetto (unspookish?) ghetto calling itself, by order, "middle class." And with that what un-reddened the ties, McCarthy, Un-American, Acts like Smith, and so How do you re-explain what "The Dictatorship of the Proletariat" means to those unconvinced of their victimization . . . by color, bribe, socialization, wish w/ media or arty academic goggledy gook?

And this is the Refreshment Mark Nowak tenders. "The photograph of the factory predicts how every one . . . will get used!" Must get Refreshed because "the place you / grew up in was going to be gone" and understand "we took care of shit" or "We couldn't make steel alone or get respect alone." These are profound ungathered ideas for the whom he reflects and speaks to, plus all of us.

He has overview, summation, & the precis of the "survivor" when the host of minds is toxic. To ask "Where are / our yards . . ." Peeping the "two doors" of (where?) America . . . from the unacknowledged fraternal citizen (not). "The white man got my job" "I have went to see" (you dig that projected precision) "is no call for colored / men." Or "A mill town is not a / goddamn residential neighborhood!"

And by positing a harked narrative, as scale- and below each, the debris of the tale, as projective verse, we are squared off with fact and fiction, as another way of seeing "America" (What dat?) the "two doors," both to nowhere!

There is this burgeoning "trend" of the double saying, above and below. What it claims is a 2-ish speech or idea or feeling or seeing? With Nowak its use is a more obvious *practice* and idea, of wd and did or will and didn't (or wont) & as a socially bounced knowing than guessing. Nowak is real and strong as you understand his "place" in all of it, trying to prove he has really dug and understood his own coming. A much needed parade.

COFFEE HOUSE PRESS FUNDERS

Coffee House Press is an independent nonprofit literary publisher. Our books are made possible through the generous support of grants and gifts from many foundations, corporate giving programs, individuals, and through state and federal support. This project received major funding from the Jerome Foundation. Coffee House Press also received support from the Minnesota State Arts Board, through an appropriation by the Minnesota State Legislature and from the National Endowment for the Arts, a federal agency; and from grants from the Elmer and Eleanor Andersen Foundation; the Buuck Family Foundation; the Bush Foundation; the Butler Family Foundation; the Grotto Foundation; the Lerner Family Foundation; the McKnight Foundation; the Outagamie Foundation; the Pacific Foundation; the John and Beverly Rollwagen Foundation; the law firm of Schwegman, Lundberg, Woessner & Kluth, P.A.; St. Paul Companies; Target, Marshall Field's, and Mervyn's with support from the Target Foundation; James R. Thorpe Foundation; West Group; the Woessner Freeman Foundation; and many individual donors.

This activity is made possible in part by a grant from the Minnesota State Arts Board, through an appropriation by the Minnesota State Legislature and a grant from the National Endowment for the Arts.

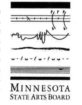

MINNESOTA
STATE ARTS BOARD

NATIONAL
ENDOWMENT
FOR THE ARTS

To you and our many readers across the country, we send our thanks for your continuing support.

Good books are brewing at coffeehousepress.org